21 DAYS OF POSITIVE AFFIRMATIONS & GRATITUDE

A PRACTICAL GUIDE TO RAISE YOUR VIBRATIONAL FREQUENCY

PP KAUR GILL

Contents

Contents

Contents

Preface

There was a time in my life when I felt like I was living my life out of a suitcase because i was into a travelling job and i had no idea how time was passing. Despite having everything a beautiful family, job, home, and all material comforts, I used to be unhappy and dissatisfied. I was living my life as a result of one ill-informed decision that led to unpleasant situations, then I became emotionally drained and made another ill-informed decision. Then came a period in my life when I began to reflect on my life decisions and realised that they were influenced either by societal pressure or by emotional upheaval, both of which are dangerous to your survival. I used to do a lot of introspection as a habit, which was making me anxious rather than getting me anywhere. In 2013 I attended a training , which set off something inside of me and began my quest for self-discovery. The power of gratitude and positive self-talk was something I learned during my exploration of the human mind, emotions, behaviour, and actions. As a result of the practise, I have developed tremendous emotional resilience and am a happier person, so I can attest to the power of affirmations and gratitude.It is proven fact that postive thoughts raises your viberational frequecy and you attract postive experiences in life.

This book is going to help you to raise your frequecy through gratitude & affirmations.This book will be your best friend for the next twenty-one days—or maybe a lifetime.Nearly every aspect of life is covered by the affirmations in this book, and the well crafted questions on gratitude encourage readers to reflect on the positive aspects of their lives.The best way to use this book is to integrate it with your regular yoga, meditation, and fitness routine.

1

Introduction

We live in a world of thoughts. Our thoughts create our experiences, and thus, we experience what we think.It is the quality of our thoughts, then, that create the quality of our life. All notable intellectuals, philosophers, and high achievers throughout history and the present have agreed that there is a "secret" that is a universal truth. This secret is based on the straightforward notion that "you are what you think". "If you get the inside right, the outside will fall into place."—Eckhart Tolle

The Link Between Thoughts, Emotions, and Behaviour

Thoughts are powerless in and of themselves; it is only when we consciously focus our attention on them that they start to take on a life of their own. We enter a new emotional state, which subsequently affects how we act, when we interact with certain thoughts. We also start to feel the feelings that these thoughts provoked. For example, if you regularly engage with the thought that you're a failure and feed more attention to it, you'll start to feel down, worthless, discouraged and perhaps even depressed. Your body's response to this is: You appear unconfident as you sulk, shrug your shoulders, and hunch your shoulders. However, if you focus on thoughts that are more empowering, they will increase your self-assurance and consequently cause a more positive emotional state. This will cause your body to respond by standing up straight, feeling optimistic, and being more energised.

Understanding thoughts as energy

The Law of conservation of energy states that – "Energy can neither be created nor be destroyed, but it can be transformed from one form to another." In its simplest form, the law says that one cannot create or destroy energy,but one can convert it from one form to another.Pretty much everything that happens in the universe obeys this fundamental law.Our enery field is also know as viberartional frequency.

It is proven fact that postive thoughts raises your viberational frequecy and you attract postive experiences in life.

We all hold energy in the form of thoughts, beliefs, emotions and memories. Therefore, even with respect to our bodies, the energy needs attention. If we are being consumed by anger, resentment, jealousy,greed,lust,hate and so on,obviously, it is serving us in some way but we know within our hearts that we can do better.Being stuck internally can lead to a number of diseases and ailments, while being stuck externally impacts our relationships, finances, professional career, and so on. The best way to deal with this, then, is to transform the energy from one form to another and just as the law says in the process, "no energy is lost"

When one transforms the energy:

Anger becomes peace.

Resentment becomes goodwill.

Greed becomes contentment.

Lust becomes detachment.

Entanglement becomes involvement.

Hate becomes acceptance at first and then love,so on and so forth, and in the process, life gets transformed. So now, the question arises as to how does one transform this energy?

There are many approaches to do this such as yoga, doing exercises, through diet, acupressure, chiro-practice, meditation etc., and different practices affect different people differently. However, for those who are analytical and like to find logic for everything- Gratitude and positive self-talk is the simplest way to transform energy.

A morning routine of affirmations and gratitude can help you focus on achieving your goals in life, change your negative thought patterns into positive ones, help you access a new belief system, but most importantly, it can bring positivity back into your life and help you regain or boost your confidence. Your reality will improve as a result of the positive energy you will generate via this practise. Every thought and every word we utter is an affirmation. Our internal dialogue is a continuous stream of affirmations. We use affirmations all the time, whether we realise it or not. With every word and thought, we affirm and create our life experiences. Our beliefs are simply habitual thought patterns that we picked up as a child. Many of them are extremely beneficial to us. Other beliefs may be limiting our ability to create the very things we want. What we want and what we believe we may be diametrically opposed. We must pay attention to our thoughts so that we can begin to eliminate those that are causing experiences in our life that we do not want. Please understand that each complaint is an affirmation of something you don't want in your life. Every time you become angry, you are confirming your desire for more anger in your life. Every time you feel like a victim, you're confirming your desire to remain a victim. If you believe that Life isn't giving you what you want, you can be certain that you will never have the benefits that Life gives to others—unless you change the way you think and speak. Positive Affirmations and gratitude are a great way to start and end each day on a positive note. If you take a few minutes each day to simply write down what you are grateful for before going to bed, you will not only go to bed thinking grateful thoughts, but you will also wake up thinking them. Affirmations and gratitude practice are the most effective tools for creating a positive mental shift. Spend 10 minutes a day for the next 21 days with this little book. I can assure you that you will notice a noticeable improvement.

2
What are Positive Affirmations?

Affirmations are almost as simple to define as they are to use. Simply put, they are positive phrases or statements that are used to counteract negative or harmful thoughts. Positive affirmation practise can be extremely simple; all you have to do is choose a phrase and repeat it to yourself. Positive affirmations can be used to motivate yourself, encourage positive changes in your life, or increase your self-esteem. Positive affirmations can be used to combat negative self-talk and replace it with more adaptive narratives if you find yourself frequently engaging in it. Affirmations can be practiced in a variety of ways, including saying them aloud, recording them, and listening to them.Write a rhyme or song and sing it while driving or going for a jog.

Is There Science -Positive Affirmations?

Science, yes. Magic, no. Positive affirmations require regular practice if you want to make lasting, long-term changes to the ways that you think and feel. The good news is that the practice and popularity of positive affirmations are based on widely accepted and well-established psychological theory. One of the key psychological theories behind positive affirmations is self-affirmation theory (Steele, 1988). So, yes, there are empirical studies based on the idea that we can maintain our sense of self-integrity by telling ourselves (or affirming) what we believe in positive ways. Very briefly, self-integrity relates to our global self-efficacy—our perceived ability to control moral outcomes and respond flexibly when our self-concept is threatened (Cohen & Sherman, 2014). So, we as humans are motivated to protect ourselves from these threats by maintaining our self-integrity.

A Look at the Research behind Affirmations The development of self-affirmation theory has led to neuroscientific research aimed at investigating whether we can see any changes in the brain when we self-affirm in positive ways. There is MRI evidence suggesting that certain neural pathways are increased when people practice self-affirmation tasks (Cascio et al., 2016). If you want to be super specific, the ventromedial prefrontal cortex—involved in positive valuation and self-related information processing—becomes more active when we consider our personal values (Falk et al., 2015; Cascio et al., 2016). The results of a study by Falk and colleagues suggest that when we choose to practice positive affirmations, we're better able to view "otherwise-threatening information as more self-relevant and valuable" (2015: 1979). As we'll see in a moment, this can have several benefits because it relates to how we process information about ourselves.

3

What does it mean to be grateful?

The word gratitude is derived from the Latin word gratia, which means grace, graciousness, or gratefulness (depending on the context). In some ways, gratitude encompasses all of these meanings. Gratitude is a thankful appreciation for what an individual receives, whether tangible or intangible. With gratitude, people acknowledge the goodness in their lives. In the process, people usually recognize that the source of that goodness lies at least partially outside themselves. As a result, being grateful also helps people connect to something larger than themselves as individuals — whether to other people, nature, or a higher power. The state of being grateful is simply defined as gratitude. It entails expressing gratitude or appreciation for something, ranging from a gift to life itself. Gratitude entails acknowledging the positive aspects of your life and how they affect you. This can range from noticing a beautiful flower on the sidewalk to feeling grateful after recovering from a serious illness.

Research on gratitude

Two psychologists, Dr. Robert A. Emmons of the University of California, Davis, and Dr. Michael E. McCullough of the University of Miami, have done much of the research on gratitude. In one study, they asked all participants to write a few sentences each week, focusing on particular topics. One group wrote about things they were grateful for that had occurred during the week. A second group wrote about daily irritations or things that had displeased them, and the third wrote about events that had affected them (with no emphasis on them being positive or negative). After 10 weeks, those who wrote about gratitude were more optimistic and felt better about their lives. Surprisingly, they also exercised more and had fewer visits to physicians than those who focused on sources of aggravation. Another leading researcher in this field, Dr. Martin E. P. Seligman, a psychologist at the University of Pennsylvania, tested the impact of various positive psychology interventions on 411 people, each compared with a control assignment of writing about early memories. When their week's assignment was to write and personally deliver a letter of gratitude to someone who had never been properly thanked for his or her kindness, participants immediately exhibited a huge increase in happiness scores. This impact was greater than that from any other intervention, with benefits lasting for a month.

You can express gratitude in many ways Gratitude exercises, such as journaling, Paying attention to the little things in life, like the birds in the trees, Telling someone you're grateful for them or for something they did, even if it was a long time ago, Doing something kind for someone in your life to express your gratitude, Meditating on the positive aspects of your life and Giving thanks through prayer.

Getting Started with Gratitude

If you want to start practising gratitude on a regular basis, there are several exercises that can help you do. Gratitude journaling is one of the extremely powerful techniques I discuss in this book.

Gratitude journaling is a technique that involves keeping a daily journal of things for which you are grateful. This is one of the most common ways to express gratitude. Recounting a favorite moment from the day, describing a special person in your life, or listing five things you're grateful for that day are all good places to start. A physical journal is recommended, However, if it is not possible It can be as simple as a phone note.

4

Benefits of practicing positive affirmations and gratitude

Positive affirmations and gratitude practise have numerous mental and physical benefits. Regular practise has been shown to have measurable health benefits.

Boosts the immune system

Improves mental health

Improved relationships

Increased optimism

Why Is It Important to Begin Each Day With a Positive Attitude?

Starting your day with a positive attitude allows you to concentrate on how you want to present yourself throughout the day. When you are feeling down and thinking negatively, you tend to focus solely on those feelings. These thoughts and feelings have the ability to dominate your mind and mood. You are more likely to have a good day if you decide to have one. Being optimistic will improve your life quality. When you are positive, you are more likely to try new things and have a broader perspective on things, and your productivity will improve because you won't be drowning in negativity. Every day, each of us has the opportunity to CHOOSE to make it a great day. You can focus on what is important in the day by focusing on what is good and not allowing negative thoughts to take over. You can focus on your goal without allowing negative thoughts to take over your mind and mood.

Why You Need A Morning Ritual?

Starting your day with a positive mindset allows you to focus on how you want to show up for the day. If you are feeling negative and have negative thoughts, you tend to focus on only those feelings. These thoughts and feelings can take over your mind and mood. Your life's worth is not determined by the worth of your circumstances. You can successfully alter the mental and emotional filters through which you perceive your life. This has an impact on the stories we tell ourselves about who we are, what we are capable of, and whether or not we can achieve our objectives. The states we frequent become the most powerful filter of all, determining whether we discover the necessary strategies for success and whether we create a story that empowers us. Change for the better is always possible, but how does one go about it? Morning rituals that can change your life do so by putting you in a positive, empowering frame of mind that you can carry with you throughout the day. One of the most important scientific discoveries has been the ability to change your emotional mood through a radical shift in your physiology, which we can begin to achieve through affirmations,gratitude and meditation.

ᛒᛒᛒ

Final Thought

Begin with baby steps to establish a daily habit. Take 10 minutes out of your day for the next 21 days to practise affirmations and gratitude journaling with this tiny book. You can also try meditation or simply pay attention to the little things in life that bring you joy. If done on a regular basis, it will most likely have a positive long-term impact on your mental health and well-being.

ᛒᛒᛒ

Simple Suggestions

1.After finishing the book, you will be able to create your own affirmations.It is entirely up to you whether to choose from the book or create your own.

2.Say these affirmations aloud and include your senses in the process (e.g., Say,hear,visualize,feel, smell)

3.Try to practice first thing in the morning before you begin your day.

ᛒᛒᛒ

5

Meditation for the Beginners

1. Sit comfortably and close your eyes, simply focus on your natural inhaling and exhaling for one minute.
2. Pay attention to your breathing. Where do you feel your breath the most? In your stomach? In your nose? Keep your focus on your inhale and exhale.
3. For another two minutes, pay attention to your breathing. Take a deep inhale, expanding your belly, and then exhale slowly, elongating the out-breath as your belly contracts.
4. Before you open your eyes, visualize whatever you have written in gratitude journal of that day and Mentally repeat at least one affirmation for the day.
5. With a gentle smile open your eyes.

6

Let's Begin

It's the little things that make a big difference

7
DAY 1- Gratitude

When you are grateful, fear disappears and abundance appears.—TONY ROBBINS

Affirmation of Gratitude

I am grateful to be alive.

I am grateful to be a part of this amazing universe.

I am grateful for the sun, the moon, the stars, and the beauty of the nature
that's all around me.

I am grateful for the blessings in my life, both big and small.

I am grateful for my family and friends.

I am grateful to have shelter and food.

I am grateful for every opportunity that comes my way.

I am grateful that I'm able to give and receive love.

I am designing a life that makes me happy, and I am in control of my
happiness.

I return to the basics of life: forgiveness, courage, gratitude, love, and
humor.

Being kind to others is very important to me, and I practise it throughout
the day.

I am grateful that I'm able to make a difference in this world.

I am grateful for all the experiences I've had in my life thus far. Gratitude
is my new way of living.

Gratitude Journal Day 1

When answering these questions, use all of your senses and become completely immersed in the process. You can either write in the book or keep a separate journal.

Question 1: Today I am grateful for............because..

Answer..

....

....

....

Question 2: What are you looking forward to doing today or tomorrow?

Answer..

....

....

....

Question 3: Describe your happiest childhood memory.

Answer..

....

....

....

8
DAY 2 - Self Esteem

"If you carry your childhood with you, you never become older." Tom Stoppard

Affirmations for Self -Esteem

My self-esteem is high because I value who I am.

I believe in myself and my abilities.

Everything I need to succeed is within me.

I release negative self-talk and do not require validation from others.

I choose to have faith in the process.

I choose to feel good about myself.

I accept and use my own power.

I am completely suitable for all situations.

I see the world through the eyes of love and acceptance.

In my world, everything is fine.

I deserve everything good, and my life is getting better by the day.

I am confident that I can find a solution to any problem.

I go through life knowing that I am safe—divinely protected and guided.

I accept others for who they are, and they accept me for who I am.

I am wonderful, and I feel fantastic.

I have the self-esteem, power, and confidence to move forward in life with ease.

Gratitude Journal Day 2

When answering these questions, use all of your senses and become completely immersed in the process. You can either write in the book or keep a separate journal.

Question 1: Today I am grateful for.............because...

Answer...

....

....

....

Question 2: What are you looking forward to doing today or tomorrow?

Answer...

....

....

....

Question 3: What is one of your favorite songs from your childhood?

What were the qualities you were praised for, as a child?

Answer...

....

....

....

9
DAY 3 - New Beginnings

"Every new beginning comes from some other beginning's end." —SENECA

Affirmations for New Beginnings

I welcome change.

I have everything I need to move ahead.

I am open to new possibilities and things are getting better by the day.

I am thankful for everything I have and everything that is to come.

I allow my blessings to come to me

I am exactly where I am supposed to be.

I am making decisions that are in my best interests.

I let go of all old patterns that are no longer useful to me.

I am willing to examine how and where I need to improve Life only provides me with positive experiences.

I am open to new and exciting changes.

I let go of any restrictions based on old negative thoughts.

I eagerly anticipate the future. Every change in my life has the potential to elevate me to a new level of comprehension.

I am always adaptable and changeable.

I am adaptable and fluid.

I am willing to push myself beyond my comfort zone.

I feel safe in the ever-changing rhythm and flow of life.

Gratitude Journal Day 3

When answering these questions, use all of your senses and become completely immersed in the process. You can either write in the book or keep a separate journal.

Question 1: Today I am grateful for............because...

Answer...

....

....

....

Question 2: What are you looking forward to doing today or tomorrow?

Answer...

....

....

....

Question 3:Write down five positive changes you've made in your life in the past.(Big or small)

Answer...

....

....

....

"The bad news is time flies. The good news is you are the pilot."- Michael Altshuler

Affirmations to Let Go

I let go of all negative thoughts from the past.

I forgive everyone from my past who has done me wrong.

I let them go with love. I let go of the need to blame anyone or anything, including myself.

I am grateful to my past self for bringing me this far.

I am healing at my own pace, and I am at peace.

I am choosing to let go of my fears.

I embrace my fears with open arms, and I overcome them.

I leave the past in the past.

My heart is wide open, I am willing to forgive.

I am now letting go of my anger in constructive ways.

I've moved past old limitations.

I am now able to express myself freely and creatively.

I let go of any lingering feelings of competition or comparison.

I am ready to move on.

Gratitude Journal Day 4

When answering these questions, use all of your senses and become completely immersed in the process. You can either write in the book or keep a separate journal.

Question 1: Today I am grateful for............because...

Answer...

....

....

....

Question 2: What are you looking forward to doing today or tomorrow?

Answer...

....

....

....

Question 3: What has been your most significant personal achievement?

Answer...

....

....

....

11

DAY 5 - Acceptance

"Develop an attitude of gratitude. Say thank you to everyone you meet for everything they do for you." BRIAN TRACY

Affirmations for Acceptance

Everybody is doing the best they can, including me.

I release the need to criticize others.

I unconditionally accept who I am.

I accept criticism and accept it is not personal.

I understand that no one is perfect, including me.

I accept my flaws. I only speak positively about those in my world.

I give myself permission to feel all of my emotions.

I give myself permission to express my emotions.

I accept all of my emotions.

I reassure my inner child that we are safe.

I am comfortable with all of my emotions.

The more honest I am, the more loved I am. My thoughts are valued.

I respect others for being different, but not necessarily incorrect, we are all connected.

I am willing to let go of all criticism patterns.

I accept myself and others.

Gratitude Journal Day 5

When answering these questions, use all of your senses and become completely immersed in the process. You can either write in the book or keep a separate journal.

Question 1: Today I am grateful for..because..

Answer..

....

....

....

Question 2: What are you looking forward to doing today or tomorrow?

Answer..

....

....

....

Question 3: What is biggest lesson you learned in childhood?

Answer..

....

....

....

12

DAY 6 - Forgiveness

"True forgiveness is when you can say 'Thank you for that experience"-OPRAH WINFREY

Affirmations for Forgiveness

I accept personal responsibility for my actions.

I am liberated.

I'm learning to forgive and let go.

My goal is to achieve inner peace.

People do their best with the information, understanding, and awareness they have at the time.

I forgive others and now design my life the way I want it to be. Forgiving makes me feel light and free.

There is no such thing as right or wrong.

I go beyond my own judgment.

I forgive myself for any regrets that I have been holding and remind myself to focus on the present.

Self-forgiveness is a choice, it is a gift of freedom that I give myself.

As I forgive myself, it becomes easier to forgive others, I allow myself to be forgiven.

I am done beating myself up for what has happened in the past.

Every day I have the power to choose, and today I choose to let go of grudges, frustrations and anger and choose to be happy.

Gratitude Journal Day 6

When answering these questions, use all of your senses and become completely immersed in the process. You can either write in the book or keep a separate journal.

Question 1: Today I am grateful for............because...

Answer...

....

....

....

Question 2: What are you looking forward to doing today or tomorrow?

Answer...

....

....

....

Question 3: What has been your most significant professional achievement?

Answer...

....

....

....

13
DAY 7 - Health

"Take care of your body. It's the only place you have to live in."— Jim Rohn

Affirmations for Health

I recognize my body as a good friend.

I adore every single cell in my body, every cell has divine intelligence.

I listen to my body and I know that its advice is valid.

I am bursting with energy and enthusiasm.

I am healthy, whole, and full of joy. I am the only person in charge of my eating habits.

I make healthy choices, the quickest way to health is to fill my mind with pleasant thoughts.

I let life and vitality pass through me.

I am thankful for my good health.

I adore life. Relaxation allows my body to repair and rejuvenate itself.

The more I unwind, the better I feel. I go for brisk walks in the sunshine to energize my body and soul.

I allow myself to be well because I love myself. My body heals quickly.

I love and accept myself at every age, each moment in life is perfect.

I lovingly take care of my body, my mind and my emotions.

Gratitude Journal Day 7

When answering these questions, use all of your senses and become completely immersed in the process. You can either write in the book or keep a separate journal.

Question 1: Today I am grateful for.............because...

Answer..

....

....

....

Question 2: What are you looking forward to doing today or tomorrow?

Answer..

....

....

....

Question 3: List 10 hobbies and activities that bring you joy.

Answer..

....

....

....

14
DAY 8 — Self Love

♡

"You yourself, as much as anybody in the entire universe, deserve your love and affection." Buddha

Affirmations for Self Love

I understand that in order for others to love me, I must first love myself.

My self-love journey begins now.

I accept and love myself, and I am safe.

I now discover how wonderful I am and I choose to love and enjoy myself.

I am worthy of my own love, and I am loved and accepted exactly as I am, right now.

My consciousness is filled with healthy, loving thoughts that manifest in my experience.

Self love is the greatest gift I can give myself.

I look great and feel great. Here I am, world—open to all that is good!

Love is a miraculous cure. In my life, loving myself has worked wonders.

I am kind, gentle, and patient with myself. This tender care is reflected in those around me.

I am part of the Universal design, I am important and loved by life itself.

I am loving and lovable and appreciate all of myself.

Gratitude Journal Day 8

When answering these questions, use all of your senses and become completely immersed in the process. You can either write in the book or keep a separate journal.

Question 1: Today I am grateful for............because..

Answer...

....

....

....

Question 2: What are you looking forward to doing today or tomorrow?

Answer...

....

....

....

Question 3: How can you pamper yourself in the next 24 hours?

Answer...

....

....

....

15

DAY 9 - Relationship

"Love is the whole thing. We are only pieces"-Rumi

Affirmations for Relationship

Love makes me feel liberated and Being in love is risk-free for me.

My partner and I look after each other and ourselves.

My partner and I are always partners on an equal footing. When I am myself, people love me.

I deserve love.Loving myself and others becomes easier with each passing day.

The more I open up to love, the more secure I feel.

My partner and I respect one another's choices.

I am now establishing a long-term, loving relationship.

I allow myself to experience intimate love.

I behave and think in a loving way to all people for I know that which I give out returns to me multiplied.

I live in harmony and balance with everyone I know.

Love fills my heart,my body, my mind,my consciousness,my very being,and radiates out from me in all directions.

Gratitude Journal Day 9

When answering these questions, use all of your senses and become completely immersed in the process. You can either write in the book or keep a separate journal.

Question 1: Today I am grateful for............because..

Answer...

....

....

....

Question 3: Who made you smile in the past 24 hours and why?

Answer...

....

....

....

Question 3: Whom have you made smile in the past 24 hours, and how?

Answer...

....

....

....

16
DAY 10 - Family

"A happy family is but an earlier heaven." – George Bernard Shaw

Affirmations for Family

I receive more love as I give more love.

My bond with my family is strong and founded on trust and love.

I am thankful for every member of my family.

My family and I are in love. My family deserves to be happy.

We share in each other's joy and success.

I support my family and my family supports me. Our happiness encourages other families to be happy as well.

I enjoy spending quality time with my family.

We set goals as a family to help our dreams come true.

I am grateful that my family accepts me for who I am.

Even when life gets in the way, I always try to make time for my family.

My family is deserving of unconditional love.

My family is always first in my life.

I have the ability to bring joy to my family.

My family deserves nothing but the best from me.

Gratitude Journal Day 10

When answering these questions, use all of your senses and become completely immersed in the process. You can either write in the book or keep a separate journal.

Question 1: Today I am grateful for............because...

Answer...

....

....

....

Question 2: What are you looking forward to doing today or tomorrow together with your family?

Answer...

....

....

....

Question 3: Describe a weird family tradition that you love and Describe a family tradition that you are most grateful for.

Answer...

....

....

....

17

DAY 11 - Friendship

*"Anything is possible when you have the right people there to support you." -
Misty Copeland*

Affirmations for Friendship

I allow myself to be a friend.

My friends are loving and supportive.

I have respect for others, and they have respect for me.

My acceptance and love for others fosters long-lasting friendships; and It is safe for me to be open.

It is safe for me to request what I desire and I express myself honestly.

Loving people fill my life, and I find it easy to express my feelings for others.

The people in my life are true reflections of myself. My world is secure and welcoming.

I am creating great memories with my friends all the time.

I choose to have only healthy relationships. All of my friends are determined and goal-oriented, just like me.

My friends and I can always rely on each other.

I deserve to have amazing people as my friends.

The best gifts I can give to everyone are a happy joyful face and loving words.

Gratitude Journal Day 11

When answering these questions, use all of your senses and become completely immersed in the process. You can either write in the book or keep a separate journal.

Question 1: Today I am grateful for............because...

Answer..

....

....

....

Question 2: What are you looking forward to doing today or tomorrow with your friends ?

Answer..

....

....

....

Question 3: Who is the one friend you can always rely on and why?

Answer..

....

....

....

18
DAY 12 – Passion

"Passion is energy. Feel the power that comes from focusing on what excites you."-Oprah Winfrey

Affirmations for Passion

I let go of all inhibitions to fully express my creativity.

Every day, I do something new or different.

I have a natural connection to the infinite creativity of the universe.

I'm grateful for the constant flow of inspiration in my life.

I have a strong drive to work hard and lead a fulfilling life.

I may inspire others by expressing myself creatively.

There is plenty of time and space for creative expression in whatever area I choose.

I am confident that I am capable of performing miracles in my life.

I enjoy expressing myself in a variety of creative ways.

I am my own special, creative, and wonderful self, and my potential is limitless.

I am a joyful, creative expression of life, and my innate creativity delights and surprises me.

I think clearly and express myself clearly.

Gratitude Journal Day 12

When answering these questions, use all of your senses and become completely immersed in the process. You can either write in the book or keep a separate journal.

Question 1: Today I am grateful for............because...

Answer...

....

....

....

Question 2: What are you looking forward to doing today or tomorrow?

Answer...

....

....

....

Question 3: What makes you happy to be alive? List 5 skills you have that most people don't possess.

Answer...

....

....

....

19
DAY 13 - Work

"The only way to do great work is to love what you do. If you haven't found it yet, keep looking. Don't settle."-Steve Jobs

Affirmations for Work

I love and enjoy my work and I am grateful.

I believe I deserve to have a successful career/business, and I accept it now.

I enjoy the work I do and the people I work with.

I am willing to seek assistance when I encounter problems on the job.

My overall happiness is reflected in the joy I find in my career.

Everyone recognizes my work and I make every experience an opportunity.

I am capable, competent, and in the ideal situation.

I look for the best in everyone and they reciprocate.

My thoughts generate a fantastic new opportunity.

I'm prepared to advance in my career now that the moment has come.

I add value to my organization and I am an asset to any organization.

I have all the skills and i have all the resources to upgrade my skills.

Gratitude Journal Day 13

When answering these questions, use all of your senses and become completely immersed in the process. You can either write in the book or keep a separate journal.

Question 1: Today I am grateful for.............because...

Answer...

....

....

....

Question 3: What is a major lesson that you learned from your job?Answer...

....

....

....

Question 3: What aspects of your job do you enjoy the most?List 5 qualities you like about yourself.

Answer...

....

....

....

20
DAY 14 - Success

"Try not to become a man of success. Rather become a man of value."- Albert Einstein

Affirmations for Success

I'm now letting the success formula pass through me and manifest in my world.

Divine Intelligence provides me with all of the ideas I can use.

I add value to the world through my work and receive value in return.

Everything I touch succeeds, and I have all of the necessary ingredients for success.

There is enough for everyone, including myself.

I develop a new sense of success.

I enter the winner's circle.

I am a Divine Prosperity magnet.

I have been blessed beyond my wildest dreams.

Riches of all kinds are drawn to me.

For me, golden opportunities abound.

Whatever I am directed to do will be successful.

Every experience teaches me something new.

Gratitude Journal Day 14

When answering these questions, use all of your senses and become completely immersed in the process. You can either write in the book or keep a separate journal.

Question 1: Today I am grateful for............because...

Answer..

....

....

....

Question 2: What are you looking forward to doing today or tomorrow?

Answer..

....

....

....

Question 3: What is a small win that you accomplished in the past 24 hours? List 5 goals you would like to accomplish in this or next year.

Answer..

....

....

....

21

DAY 15 - Financial Abundance & Prosperity

"True prosperity is appreciating what you have." Bill Ferguson

Affirmations for Financial Abundance & Prosperity

I am grateful to live in a loving, abundant, and harmonious universe.

I am a money magnet. Prosperity in all forms is drawn to me.

I am deserving of money in the bank.

My earnings are steadily increasing.

Today, money comes to me in both predictable and unexpected ways.

My credit score is improving all the time.

I manage my finances well.

I always have enough of what I need.

I have as much money as I am willing to accept.

I love and bless all of my bills. I always pay them on time.

I am always financially secure.

I'm looking forward to my retirement.

I enjoy saving and spending in moderation, and I give myself permission to prosper.

Gratitude Journal Day 15

When answering these questions, use all of your senses and become completely immersed in the process. You can either write in the book or keep a separate journal.

Question 1: Today I am grateful for............because.............

Answer...

....

....

....

Question 2: What are you looking forward to do today or tomorrow?

Answer...

....

....

....

Question 3: What is a recent purchase that has added value to your life?List items that you take for granted and that might not be available to people in other parts of the world (e.g., clean water, electricity, etc.).

Answer...

....

....

....

22

DAY 16 - Compulsive Habits

"People often say that motivation doesn't last. Neither does bathing. That's why we recommend it daily." – Zig Ziglar

Affirmations for Compulsive Habits

I am at peace, and I am completely adequate in all situations.

I relieve stress by deep breathing and I feed myself with my own love.

I have the ability, strength, and knowledge to handle any situation in my life.

I let go of the need to be perfect.

I am sufficient in my current state. I am open to inner wisdom.

I recognise my patterns and make changes without shame or guilt.

I understand that awareness is the first step toward healing or change.

Every day, I become more aware.

I relax into Life's flow and allow Life to provide everything I need easily and comfortably.

I am willing to think differently about myself and my life; and I love, appreciate, and respect myself; I am gentle and kind to myself as I grow and change; and No one, place, or thing has power over me.

I am liberated.

Gratitude Journal Day 16

When answering these questions, use all of your senses and become completely immersed in the process. You can either write in the book or keep a separate journal.

Question 1: Today I am grateful for............because.............

Answer..

....

....

....

Question 2: What are you looking forward to do today or tomorrow?

Answer..

....

....

....

Question 3: Describe an experience that was painful but made you a stronger person.What is your favorite habit, and why it is an important part of your daily routine?

Answer..

....

....

....

23

DAY 17 - Stress Free Life

"Stress acts as an accelerator: it will push you either forward or backward, but you choose which direction."-Chelsea Erieau

Affirmations for Stress Free Life

I let go of all fear and doubt, and my life becomes simple and easy; I create a stress-free environment for myself.

I release any tension in my shoulders and relax all of my neck muscles.

I take slow, deep breaths in and out, relaxing more and more with each one.

I am a capable individual who can handle any situation that arises.

I am calm and focused. Every day, I feel more secure.

I am even-tempered and emotionally balanced; I am at ease with myself and with others.

I am safe when I express my feelings.

I can remain calm in any situation.

I have great relationships with my friends, family, and coworkers. I am grateful.

I have faith in myself to handle any problems that arise during the day.

I am making positive changes in all aspects of my life, and I have the strength to remain calm in the face of change.

I know I am divinely protected.

Gratitude Journal Day 17

When answering these questions, use all of your senses and become completely immersed in the process. You can either write in the book or keep a separate journal.

Question 1: Today I am grateful for............because............

Answer..

....

....

....

Question 2: What are you looking forward to do today or tomorrow?

Answer..

....

....

....

Question 3: Describe a recent time when you truly felt at peace.What is your favorite way to enjoy nature (e.g., walking in the woods/garden, hiking in the mountains)?

Answer..

....

....

....

24

DAY 18 - Inner self

❤

"It is imperative you stay in touch with your inner self so you don't lose the essence of who you truly are."- Omoakhuana Anthonia

Affirm to connect with Inner self

My being is greater than the present moment. Every day, I completely rely on my intuition because I am the master of my own thoughts.

I am at peace with myself and have complete faith in myself.

I am aware of everything that is going on around me.

I am the architect of my own life, and I am mentally and physically balanced.

I am at home in my body, and I am reclaiming my power.

I accept my individuality. Every day, I get closer to my true self.

I aware of my mistakes and learn from them. Every day, I learn valuable lessons from myself. I believe in my ability to make sound decisions.

I am divinely guided towards my higher purpose.

I am fully present, focused, and grounded in this moment.

Gratitude Journal Day 18

When answering these questions, use all of your senses and become completely immersed in the process. You can either write in the book or keep a separate journal.

Question 1: Today I am grateful for.............because.............

Answer...

....

....

....

Question 2: What are you looking forward to do today or tomorrow?

Answer...

....

....

....

Question 3: Describe your favorite smell,favorite sound, favorite sight, favorite taste and describe your favorite sensation.

Answer...

....

....

....

25
DAY 19 - Spirituality

"Everything amazing about the universe is inside of you, and the two are inseparable." — Carl Sagan

Affirmations for Spirituality

I am an extension of the Universe.

I am a divine being who is linked to the Universe.

I am a spirit going through a human experience.

I have access to source energy at all times.

My true strength is found in the present moment.

I am one with the Universe that gave birth to me.

I believe in the divine plan of the Universe and am on my way to enlightenment.

I am linked to the Universe's wisdom.

I'm willing to follow the Universe's lead.

I am in sync with Universal power.

I remove all impediments to my spiritual connection.

I've let go of my fear and am now ready to realign.

I'm ready to lift the spiritual realm's veil and I'm willing to learn through love.

I call on my higher power for wisdom and guidance in all situations.

I am connected to the wisdom of the universe.

I have a deep sense of inner peace that is always within me, no matter what happens.

I am filled with God's grace, peace, and joy.

Gratitude Journal Day 19

When answering these questions, use all of your senses and become completely immersed in the process. You can either write in the book or keep a separate journal.

Question 1: Today I am grateful for............because......................................

Answer...

....

....

....

Question 2: What are you looking forward to do today or tomorrow?

Answer...

....

....

....

Question 3: List 5 miraculous events that occurred in your life.

Answer...

....

....

....

26

DAY 20 - World Peace

"Be the Change You Wish to See in the World."-Mahatma Gandhi

Affirmation for World Peace

Today, I reflect on what peace means to me and Peace in the world begins with me.

Every day, I show up for the world and everyone in it with kindness, compassion, love, and care.

I live in a lovely world filled with peace and kindness. On Earth, there is increasing joy and happiness every day.

I choose to believe in a better tomorrow.

I am entitled to a clear sky above my head. Everyone on the planet deserves a calm sky.

I recognise that spreading violence and hatred only leads to more violence and hatred.

I'm doing everything I can to channel my negative energy into creative projects in order to let it all go.

I affirm that there is enough water, food, shelter, and love on Earth for everyone who requires it.

The higher power has kept me safe and protected. Nothing and no one can have a negative impact on me.

I'm doing my best to be kind to people and the environment. I am motivating others to do the same.

Today, I cause a positive ripple effect by doing something nice for someone else.

Gratitude Journal Day 20

When answering these questions, use all of your senses and become completely immersed in the process. You can either write in the book or keep a separate journal.

Question 1: Today I am grateful for............because...

Answer..

....

....

....

Question 2: What are you looking forward to do today or tomorrow?

Answer..

....

....

....

Question 3: Write about a recent time when a stranger did something nice for you or you did something nice for a stranger.

Answer..

....

....

....

27
Day 21 – Personal Affirmations

Congratulations on completing The 20-Days. You have dedicated the last twenty days to focusing on positivity, instead of surrounding yourself with negativity. Even if you've only journaled for a few minutes daily, you have discovered what it's like to recognize the good in the world.

"Freedom is not given to us by anyone; we have to cultivate it ourselves. It is a daily practice… No one can prevent you from being aware of each step you take or each breath in and breath out." – Thich Nhat Hanh

Your Personal Affirmations

Your Personal Affirmations Today, write your own affirmations. You can create your own statements or use this book as a guide. Read them aloud with zeal. Create a song out of your affirmations and sing it joyfully. Allow your mind to replay these affirmations throughout the day. Most importantly, include all five of your senses in the process.

I am..

....

....

....

....

....

....

....

....

....

....

....

....

....

Gratitude Journal Day 21

When answering these questions, use all of your senses and become completely immersed in the process. You can either write in the book or keep a separate journal.

Question 1: Today I am grateful for............because......................................

Answer...

....

....

....

Question 2: What are you looking forward to do today or tomorrow?

Answer...

....

....

....

Question 3: What impact do you believe you can have on your life if you continue your affirmation and gratitude journaling practise for the next year?

Answer...

....

....

....

Conclusion

Embracing good can have a transformative effect on your life. As mentioned before, learning how to be more grateful and affirming the good will raise your viberational frequency : Increase your happiness. Improve your mental health. Allow you to savor every positive experience. Help you cope with major life challenges. Create a sense of resilience in how you approach challenging experiences. Boost your self-esteem and Strengthen your relationships. Foster empathy for others and provide a better night's sleep.

After journaling for the past Twenty days, you've probably experienced many of the benefits of affirmations and gratitude. Not only is it a great habit that improves your life, it can also have a positive spillover effect on the people around you. Now, we encourage you to frequently reread this journal. This practice will act as a reminder about all the amazing things that you have right now—not in some distant, faraway future.Practicing affirmations will create a postive cognitive shift. Finally, we would love to hear about your experience with this journal, and which prompts you found most useful. If you'd like to share your thoughts feel free to email us at ppkaurgill@gmail.com

Here are some things I can help with:

1. How to go from feeling like a VICTIM to feeling EMPOWERED

2. The different stages of MANIFESTATION

3. Help you be ALIGNED WITH YOUR HIGHER SELF so you can go from reacting to responding to situations.

4. Help you manage your GUILT and ANGER

5. Connect you to the DIVINE ENERGY, truly tap into that INNER SELF so you become UNSTOPPABLE

6. Help you SET CLEAR BOUNDARIES around people who drain your energy

7. INCREASE YOUR MOTIVATION for living LIFE

My approach is a combination of metaphysics and spirituality. If you know of anyone who could use my expertise,please share the website link. https://ppkaurgill.com/ If you have any questions at all, reply and let me know on ppkaurgill@gmail.com.

Thanks for investing both your time and money. We hope you enjoyed the journey of discovering the unique power of positive mindset. Cheers, (Ppkaur Gill)

References Source:
https://www.health.harvard.edu/
https://positivepsychology.com/daily-affirmations/
https://www.ncbi.nlm.nih.gov/pmc/articles/PMC4814782/

❧❧❧

<h1 style="text-align:center">About The Author</h1>

PP Kaur Gill is an aviation trainer and an Intrapreneurial mindset coach. This book is inspired by her own journey of transformation. She believes that practicing gratitude and reflecting on things that you're grateful for, can really help to quiet or shift underlying negative self-talk.Her self-discovery enabled her to change her life, going from a struggling working mother to a successful life coach and aviation professional. A positive outlook gives us greater awareness and enables us to lead balanced lives. Spending 21 Days with this book will undoubtedly result in lasting mental change.

♡♡♡